I0429136

TABLE OF CONTENTS

The Color of White
It Is Not Simply an Absence of Color
©Copyright 2012 by Dr. Leland Benton

DISCLAIMER AND TERMS OF USE AGREEMENT:

(Please Read This Before Using This Book)

This information is for educational and informational purposes only. The content is not intended to be a substitute for any professional advice, diagnosis, or treatment.

The authors and publisher of this book and the accompanying materials have used their best efforts in preparing this book.

The authors and publisher make no representation or warranties with respect to the accuracy, applicability, fitness, or completeness of the contents of this book. The information contained in this book is strictly for educational purposes. Therefore, if you wish to apply

Introduction – The Whiteness of Chalk

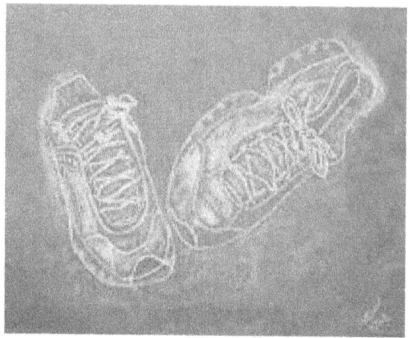

In an essay titled "A Piece of Chalk," G. K. Chesterton described one of his favorite childhood pastimes: drawing with chalk on brown paper.

He preferred brown paper to white because the colors of the chalk stand out more vividly against its rough, dark background.

The white one is the most essential piece of chalk in his collection. "One of the wise and awful truths which this brown-paper art reveals, is this, that white is a color.

It is not a mere absence of color; it is a shining and affirmative thing, as fierce as red, as definite as black."

I, too, have been guilty of thinking of white as an absence of color; in fact, white light includes colors of every other wavelength.

Wisdom is knowing what to do next

Virtue is doing it

DAVID STARR JORDAN

Chesterton provides a parallel between our mistaken thinking about the color white and our mixed up perspective on virtue. "The chief assertion of religious morality is that white is a color.

Virtue is not the absence of vices or the avoidance of moral dangers; virtue is a vivid and separate thing, like pain or a particular smell."

Have you too thought of virtue as the mere absence of vice?

In a study on the subject of pride, one of the participants asked if we were going to also study humility. "Oh, no," I responded, "If you can conquer pride, you've achieved humility."

However, after more study on the subject and a few more years of battling my own pride convinced me that I was dead wrong on this issue. It is only by pursuing the positive fruit of humility that we can ever hope to battle pride.

Humility is not the mere absence of pride any more than white is the absence of color. Humility is a "vivid and separate thing," and a prize worth pursuing.

It is only when we learn humility to think on things greater than ourselves that we will be able to abandon our pride.

C. S. Lewis' "The Weight of Glory" notes a similar misconception…
"If you asked twenty good men today what they thought the highest of the virtues, nineteen of them would reply, Unselfishness.

But if you had asked almost any of the great Christians of old, he would have replied, Love.

You see what has happened? A negative term has been substituted for a positive...."

We should pay careful attention to the avoidance of substituting negatives for positives. When God commanded his people to be holy, He did not base his command first and foremost on the detestability of sin. He grounded this command in his own character, saying "You shall be holy because I am holy."

God hates and abhors what is unholy, but this abhorrence springs from his delight in what is good and true, namely Himself. Like Him, we should not look at the joyful pursuit of holiness as the wearisome extermination of vice.

We should also cling to what is good and not merely hate what is evil. In doing so, we move from the defensive to the offensive, a move that is a major turning point in the winning of any war.

This book is about racism, bigotry, and the results of both. It addresses the fact that racism is alive and well in America. It isn't just about white versus black; it isn't about white versus, brown, red, yellow, or whatever.

By its own definition, it is not a mere absence of color and because of this very definition, white could not be its own color without other colors standing alongside of it.

In the visual world of color there cannot be any racism since white must contain all the colors of every other wavelength. It needs the other colors in order to be white.

Can this not also be true in real life?

It is all about addressing the fact that we all need each other and maybe like siblings in a family, we may have our disagreements but as siblings age, many of the arguments go away.

We cut our teeth on the racial tensions of the 1960s. The riots sparked by Rodney King beating in the early 70s should have taught us what he pleaded for us to do, "Can't we all just get along?"

As the country ages, we should be able to tackle this problem of racial prejudice and move on, but we are not doing this.

Why? This book examines the "WHY". It examines us as a country. But most of all it asks one very important question.

Why Not?

Why not learn to be "one nation under God, indivisible, with liberty and justice for all."

Yes, white is not a mere absence of color; it was never meant to be!

Chapter 1 – The Story of Kei

Racial prejudice came to me early in my lifetime. It occurred in high school. The year was 1969.

In high school I had met a Japanese girl. Her name was Kei and she was beautiful and tiny and she liked me. We liked each other almost instantly and we became inseparable.

At recess, we sat together and at lunch we ate together. After school, we studied in the library. I am convinced that I got through high school physics only because of Kei. She was brilliant.

We began dating but because she worked at her father's nursery, she would meet me at local restaurants rather than I pick her up at home or work. I didn't think anything of it but I would soon learn that Kei was harboring a secret.

I became aware of the secret one Friday evening as we were eating a pizza. I looked up at Kei and she went white and literally began to tremble. I looked over to where she was staring and there stood an elderly Japanese couple and behind them five young teenage Japanese boys.

The couple looked sad; the boys looked angry. Suddenly, the elderly gentlemen spat out Japanese in rapid staccato. Kei responded angrily in Japanese and in tears. This went on for just a few minutes ending with Kei jumping up and leaving with the five young Japanese boys.

I would soon learn that the elderly couple was Kei's parents and the boys were her brothers. I looked at Kei's father and he said in halting English and almost in a whisper, "We are a traditional Japanese family; we do not allow our women to marry outside our race. You have not done anything wrong, but Kei knows better. My wife and I hope you will honor our wishes and not date Kei. She has a very good future ahead of her and will have little time for dating and men."

With that, Kei's father and mother slid out of the booth, bowed and walked away. I never said a word; I just watched them walk away.

Candidly, I didn't know what to say; I didn't really understand what had just happened. I was aware racial tension existed but it had never affected me.

That changed quickly on that Friday evening at Shakey's Pizza Parlor.

In school the following Monday, I couldn't get close to Kei because she was guarded by her five brothers. I had one class with her – physics – and she never showed up. I soon learned she had been transferred to another class.

This went on for over a week and then one day while I was sitting eating a sandwich a girl brushed by me and dropped a note in my lap. I will never forget what it said and I still have the note tucked away in my bible, "Harry, my family holds too many silly traditions. They have embarrassed me and you and for this I apologize. Even as I see you across the quad and I see you look back, I would find it difficult to look you in the eye because of this embarrassment. I feel like a prisoner; my brothers surround me to make sure we do not make contact. I ask you to forgive me and my family. Someday we will meet again…Love Always, Kei"

I saw Kei everyday across the quad looking sad surrounded by her brothers. One day, her older brother Kenji saw me staring and walked up to me. He said, "My brothers and I will never allow you near our sister so you had better take your eyes and look elsewhere..." I never allowed him to finish his sentence. I grabbed Kenji by the neck and began beating him. I had more than 50 lbs on Kenji; I was also on the gymnastic team and strong as a bull. Tiny little Kenji never had a chance; even as his brothers, who were smaller, ran over to help him, I easily laid all five of them out on the pavement and then simply walked away.

That little episode earned me a three day expulsion from school. I was angry but I didn't know what I was angry about. My dad sat with me and asked me what had happened and I told him everything. He shook his head in understanding and just said, "Move on son; some things in life cannot be explained."

I knew one thing; I was upset with myself that I had hurt Kei's brothers. I didn't know what came over me; I just exploded in a fury. Kenji took the worst of my beating; he had a broken nose and a broken wrist. His brothers looked like they had gotten run over by a truck.

When I returned to school I no longer could see Kei in the quad. I soon learned that they had moved their location and her brothers were quick to stay away from me. In fact, just about every Japanese in the school stayed away from me. They were afraid of me and who could blame them.

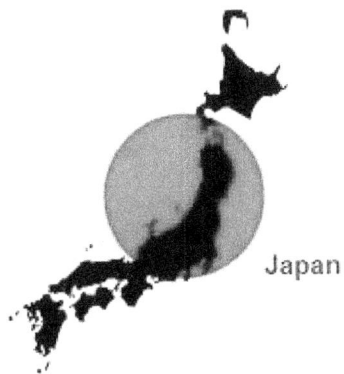

Japan

In my naivety, I missed Kei. We had a good amount of fun together and it all came to a crashing halt without warning. My anger continued to seethe. I was a very angry young man and found myself one afternoon after school driving to Kei's father's nursery.

As I walked in, Kei looked up from the counter as her brothers gathered around their father. Her father signaled for everyone to remain where they were and he walked over to talk to me.

He began, "I hope you are not here to repeat what happened at school. I apologize to you. My son Kenji should not have threatened you. I see no reason for violence and it is still my hope that you will understand my wishes in this matter."

I replied, "I didn't come here to fight; I came here to talk with you face to face. You embarrassed me and Kei in front of our school. Your son, Kenji decided to make it worse when he came over and threatened me. I, too, apologize for hurting your sons, but if you are big enough

15

to threaten another person you should learn how to fight first. I am trying to understand your wishes but you are no longer in Japan. This is America and you shouldn't expect Americans to understand your ways. I heard what you said at the pizza parlor and my response is that you are presumptuous. I am 17-years old and marriage is not on my mind. Kei and I simply like one another and she helps me with physics. I am here to tell you that I will continue to see Kei and if your sons try to stop me I will hurt them again."

Kei's father listened carefully and nodded his head. He turned to look at Kei and motioned for her to come over. She walked very slowly with her head down. Her father spoke, "You heard what this young man said?"

Kei looked up but could only nod her head.

"You know your mother and my wishes in this matter, correct?"

Again Kei just nodded.

"Do you wish to see this young man and help him with physics?"

Kei smiled for the first time and then said, "Yes."

Kei's father looked at me and then back at Kei, "See to it that both of you do not fall in love, understand?"

I could only nod; Kei barked something in Japanese and bowed to her father.

"You have my permission to see one another." With that he too bowed and walked away and left Kei and I together.

I couldn't trust myself to speak so I just muttered, "See you in school, Kei," and began to walk away. She followed me to my car holding my hand and gave me a kiss on my cheek. I don't know if her father or brothers saw this happen but if they did I had a mental image of them all committing Hari Kari and falling on samurai swords.

Kei and I were once again inseparable up and until graduation. We lost track of one another after graduation. I was drafted and went to war. I would soon learn that Kei went off to Stanford and would earn a doctorate in nuclear physics. Why not; she always was brilliant in physics.

My story doesn't end here. In 1972 I came home from the war, and enrolled in UCLA. I no longer thought much about Kei; my head was buried in my school work and the war had replaced good memories with bad. I completed my graduate studies in 1980 and this was the same year as our 10-year reunion.

I had married in 1978 and a week before my reunion, my wife had given birth to our first daughter. I went to the reunion by myself and who should be standing in the middle of the room staring at me...yep, it was Kei and she hadn't changed one bit in 10-years. I was amazed that the woman looked identical as to when I left her at graduation.

Kei immediately ran up to me jabbering away asking question after question. Kei had never married; she was a nuclear physicist at Livermore Laboratories in Livermore, California. Her parents still exercised control over her and her brothers were still around watching her but living away from her home in Los Angeles, she had finally obtained a good amount of freedom.

Kei was happy for me that I had married and had a baby daughter. I showed her all of my pictures and I could see there was no remorse; she was truly happy for me. She said she would always remember me standing up to her father and telling him that no one would stop me from seeing her. I asked her why she had never married and she said quite frankly there were no Japanese men like me.

I left the reunion with her words still in my head. Looking back, ten years later, it all seemed so silly. Racism denied a good man a fine woman like Kei. All because of some outdated tradition that was as racist as you could get, Kei was growing old alone.

Where was the sense in that?

The heart truly is a lonely hunter!

Postscript: In 1990, at our 20-year class reunion, I looked for Kei but did not see her. I was disappointed because my wife was with me and I had wanted her to meet Kei. After about an hour I looked up and saw Kenji walking towards me. He was older and fatter now but there was no mistaking it was Kenji. He bowed and asked politely if he could talk to me. We went off to the side where he informed me that Kei had died in childbirth 2-years before. She had never married but wanted children so she had used a sperm bank to get pregnant. She asked Kenji before she died to make sure I knew she always loved me. Kenji hugged me then bowed and left. My wife looked at me and walked up to ask if anything was wrong. I told her what Kenji had said and then asked if she would mind if we went home. She kissed me with tear-filled eyes as she nodded her head.

Racism pays an exacting price! It is a demanding master. It is cruel and takes what does not belong to it. In the case of Kei, it took her life. In others, it steals love, honor and self worth.

Chaim Potok, a great Jewish author wrote this:

"There is an old story about what God said to Moses when he was about to die, "You have toiled and labored, now you are worthy of rest."

"We live less than the time it takes to blink an eye, if we measure our lives against eternity. What value is there to human life?

"A blink in itself is nothing but the eye is something.

"A span of life is nothing, but the man who lives that span is something.

"He can fill that span with meaning so its quality is immeasurable though its quantity may be insignificant. Meaning is not given automatically to life. A life of meaning is worthy of rest."

Kei was beautiful; she was brilliant and for a brief moment in my life, Kei shared herself with me in conversation, knowledge and laughter. But she died only brushing up against love.

I cannot honestly say what meaning Kei's life had. I truly wonder what her family thought and how they feel that Kei died alone. She died alone for the sake of an outdated tradition.

It truly makes you wonder.

Racism has no empathy; its goal is segregation and nothing will be allowed to stand in its way.

If the heart is truly a lonely hunter, maybe it should declare open hunting season on racism.

Chapter 2 – White is as Fierce as Red and as Definite as Black

The most essential piece of chalk in his collection is the white one. He writes, "One of the wise and awful truths which this brown-paper art reveals, is this, that white is a color. It is not a mere absence of color; it is a shining and affirmative thing, as fierce as red, as definite as black." – G. K. Chesterton

White versus Black – are we still debating this racial subject? Really?

As I write this, the presidential election is in full swing with Obama being charged with using the race card over and over again.

Attorney General Holder is being charged with contempt of Congress and the Black Caucus is screaming racism.

In Florida, George Zimmerman, a member of neighborhood watch, is awaiting trial for killing a black youth, Treyvon Martin.

African Americans now constitute nearly 1 million of the total 2.3 million incarcerated populations.

African Americans are incarcerated at nearly six times the rate of whites.

Together, African American and Hispanics comprise 58% of all prisoners even though African Americans and Hispanics make up approximately one quarter of the US population.

If African American and Hispanics were incarcerated at the same rates of whites, today's prison and jail populations would decline by approximately 50%.

Racism continued to rear its ugly head in my life. After my 20-year class reunion and learning the news that Kei had died, I returned to my practice of counseling as a behavioral science doctor.

I placed Kei deep within the reaches of my heart, in a special place where I could remember only good things and I buried the rest with Kei.

Within my practice, I spent a good deal of my professional time working for the courts. It quickly became apparent to me that there was a glaring dichotomy that existed between the number of white inmates and the number of other inmates from various minorities.

I often wonder to this day if I am the only person on the planet that is aware of this dichotomy.

As a doctor, I am constantly aware of the fact that I didn't create this situation, but I am forced to work within it. This keeps me sane; otherwise, I too would turn into a hateful person.

In my practice, simply put, I deal with the unlovable. Society, in general, has spurned these people for whatever reason and being ostracized, they are determined to fight back with whomever or whatever has caused their pain.

Inmates assign various causes to their pain. It can be individuals, situations, organizations, and more.

But one thing is for certain, they blame someone or something for the way their lives have turned out.

Part of my job is identifying those inmates that can be helped. Not everyone believes they need help; not everyone will accept help.

One such person that crossed my paths was Danny. Here was a powerfully built black man serving 25-years on a rape charge.

In numerous conversations with Danny, he told me he was convicted for something he didn't do. He said that the prosecutor in his case lied, that he wasn't even in town at the time of the rape.

I looked in to Danny's case and discovered that DNA evidence could exonerate Danny. I pulled some favors and got some evidence released for DNA sampling and within 3-weeks; the results came back exonerating Danny.

Oddly enough, the man who actually committed the rape was serving time in the exact same prison as Danny, although I didn't tell Danny this information.

It took another 4-weeks to get Danny released. He came out of prison angry and a little lost. I asked Danny if he had any plans. His response was this, "Do you want to know what I want to do or what I will do, doc?"

My reply, "Both!"

"I want to kill that prosecutor that lied and took 15-years of my life but what I will do is find a job and try to stay out of trouble."

"How long do you intend to hold the anger inside of you," I asked.

Danny looked up with those piercing black eyes, "The anger keeps me going. It is my strength. It is all I have left, doc."

I found Danny a place to live. It was a studio apartment next to the bus lines. As I drove Danny to his new apartment, I thought about his words. In the weeks that followed, I got Danny a job working in a bottling plant. Danny could fix any type of machinery and the bottling plant was close enough to his apartment so that he could walk to and from work.

One day, as I was checking on Danny, I asked him how he was doing. He informed me that a black female cop named Clorice Johnson had come to his work and asked to see him. Immediately alert, I asked him what she wanted.

Danny's response shocked me. "She said she checks on all sex offenders in her area and she just wanted me to know that she was watching me."

Then Danny said something that was totally over the top, "She says I have to piss test three times per week."

My response, "Really? I guess she didn't get the word that you were exonerated.

You are not a registered sex offender nor are you under any type of probation.

I will speak to her, Danny. Sit tight until I get back to you."

I spoke to Clorice Johnson at her office in City Hall and asked her what she was doing.

I informed her that she had no jurisdiction over Danny and could not order him to do anything.

Her response, "Tell me doctor; you aren't some bleeding heart white do-gooder attempting to assuage the white race's feelings for hundreds of years of racism and bigotry, are you?"

"Maybe I am or maybe I am just doing my job. The system took 15-years of this man's life and he doesn't deserve what you are doing."

"Doctor, I am one of those cops that place little credence in DNA testing. I believe it is flawed and since this man is in my area I intend to watch him."

"You may watch him all you like but please do not attempt to order him to do anything, Ms. Johnson. And if you continue to harass the man I will go to his judge with this matter."

"My, my, my you are one uppity white man," she taunted. "Your response tells me this man has something to hide. This meeting is over, doctor."

Two days after our meeting I received a phone call that Danny was arrested on another rape charge. I went to see Danny to get the facts and knew without checking that Clorice Johnson was the arresting officer.

Danny had an ironclad alibi. He had been at work and his boss had vouched for him but Ms. Johnson arrested him anyway. He had fit the description and was identified by the rape victim in a line up.

I went to see the judge and informed him of the conversation I had with Ms. Johnson. In the arraignment hearing the judge questioned Ms. Johnson and informed her that over a dozen people had written him letters stating emphatically that Danny had been at work with them. He also informed her that DNA testing was accepted by the courts and was more reliable than any identification in a lineup. He then dismissed the case and admonished Ms. Johnson telling her to leave this man alone.

I have to tell you here and now that you had never seen an angrier black woman than Clorice Johnson. Outside of the courtroom she literally hissed at me, "You won this one doctor, but I am going to make it my life goal to put that rapist behind bars. You made it personal today."

Danny heard what she said and just shook his head. "This would be easier, doc if she was a white woman. This isn't gonna end, is it, doc?"

In the weeks that followed, Danny returned to work and his little studio apartment. I kept in close contact with him daily to be sure he wasn't being harassed. He informed me that he had not seen Ms. Johnson at all. Unfortunately, this story doesn't end on a happy note. Two months after the dismissed arraignment, Clorice Johnson was gunned down in a drive by shooting in front of her home. She was dead on arrival at the hospital and once again Danny was a suspect but he was not arrested. And once again his co-workers vouched for him being at work.

When I went to see Danny, I asked him if he was okay and he said he was fine. He then informed me very nonchalantly that he had murdered Clorice Johnson and he thought I had a right to know.

I simply asked him why and his response was, "She had told the both of us that she would not rest until she saw me behind bars. Before I went away for something I didn't do; this time I wanted to make sure I went away for something I did do."

"Why, Danny, when you are doing so well getting back your life. Why did you do this?"

Danny looked at me long and hard. It was like he was fighting within himself to tell me some deep secret.

"Doc, DNA evidence cleared me in my rape case and it is true I never raped that girl. But the man who did was serving time for another crime in the same prison as me. He did rape her; I know because I was there and would have raped her too but he got too rough and knocked her out. I am not the innocent man you think I am. Clorice Johnson was just as evil as me but with a badge. And that made her more evil. I deserve to go back to prison but I will go back knowing that Clorice Johnson won't hurt anybody else."

Danny's revelation stunned me; he could see that I was having a difficult time coming to grips with his words. "Doc, you are a good man and I could easily skate out from under this with my alibi but at least I learned from you to face life head-on and stand accountable for my actions. I owe you for that, doc."

Both of us were silent as I drove Danny to the police station to turn himself in. Once again hate and bigotry claimed more than one victim. Lives had been ended and/or destroyed.

Could we ever learn to all get along?

Postscript: Danny pleaded guilty to the murder of Clorice Johnson. He was sentenced to death and is on death row awaiting execution. He has waved all his rights to appeal.

Chapter 3 - It's Innocence When It Charms Us; it is Ignorance When it Doesn't!

It's innocence when it charms us

There are many things in this world that charm us; things that are cute, cuddly, interesting and things that make us perceive something that isn't real.

As I write this, a news article on Yahoo news, reports of a rogue bottlenose dolphin that has bitten three people in Lake Pontchartrain in Louisiana. Dolphins are cute and thanks to the 60s TV series "Flipper" (1964-1967) people perceive them to be safe animals.

Nothing can be farther from the truth; dolphins of all types can be and are highly aggressive. And let's not forget that orcas or "killer whales" are the largest dolphins.

My point is this: we perceive many things that charm us to be friendly, safe, and much more but the reality is quite different.

It's innocence when it charms us; it is ignorance when it doesn't!

One of the many hats I wear in my company is Chief Forensics Investigator for ForensicsNation.com. My behavioral science background serves me well since I personally specialize in child predation cases.

One of the most diabolical child predator cases I worked on occurred a few years back. What make this case highly unusual is that the child predator was a woman.

By far, most child predators are male but women make up the worst! Another really weird factor is that this woman was 81-years old and not one I would easily believe would be computer savvy but "Grandma Doom" as she became known as was not only computer savvy, she did not do anything to conceal her identity and was very careful not to violate the law.

Her modus operandi was befriending teenagers in teen chat rooms as a grandmotherly figure and then engaging them with a grandmotherly form of cyber-bullying.

Oh, she was good…real good and in the end we could only block her access to teen chat rooms and make it perfectly known to her that we were constantly watching her.

Thankfully, and I know this sounds very surreal, she died. We were never able to pin any crime on her; she was that careful but she left in her wake of cyber-bullying some severely messed up kids.

*****

With the advent and acceptance of social media, kids of all ages are online doing things that kids do online such as sharing photos, talking smack, music, videos and more.

Today's kids are growing up in an era of high technology and they have no problem being computer savvy and this fact, tied to their use of cellphones, gives them tremendous communication abilities but at the same time sets them up for some serious predation.

In a small village-like town outside of Ensenada, Mexico, off the highway that bisects farm communities and connects the west coast of Mexico to the east coast right above the town of San Felipe, lived two Mexican kids, Reuben Chavez, age 16 and his sister Sonja Chavez, age 14.

These two kids lived with their aunt, an elderly woman in a tiny but upscale house, because their mother and father had illegally immigrated to the United States. Their hope was to join their parents in the Imperial Valley of California and they communicated with them using chat rooms and email.

They would walk to Ensenada every evening to an Internet cafe just to go online and speak to their parents. This is how they stayed connected with their parents and this is how Antonio Rivas found them.

Rivas was a registered sex offender who had already served time for a variety of child predation crimes. He lurked in teen chat rooms and scoured the net daily for victims.

The odd thing about Rivas was that he only preyed on Latino children. In 31-years of being a forensics investigator, I have never witnessed anything like this.

When we first targeted Rivas and busted him for his first child predation crimes, I admit this threw us off. He was the first child predator to display this trait and we haven't seen it since.

Racism is practiced within a given ethnic race and is not just reserved as a battle between races. And the case with Reuben, Sonja and Rivas was blatant racism because Rivas harbored one dark secret; he was an epileptic and when growing up, he was subject to other kid's taunts and bullying. He grew up hating Latino children and this hatred manifested itself into child predation.

Reuben and Sonja liked to visit Latino chat rooms. Both kids did not come from a peasant background. They were educated and both spoke English quite well.

As with all registered and convicted child predators, my company tracks their cyber-movements; where they go online, who they talk to, what is being said, etc. With the chat room's permission, we are able to place a computer program into their software that enables us to do a good many things of which I cannot speak about for security reasons.

The initial conversation between Rivas and the Chavez kids can best be described as friendly. Rivas told them that he was an immigration attorney working to get illegal immigrants "green cards" that enabled them to work legally in the US.

As you can imagine, this was of tremendous interest to both Reuben and Sonja and they struck up a lengthy conversation with Rivas, unaware that he was a predator and unaware that Rivas' was lying.

Rivas was not a stupid man; he knew which buttons to push to draw the kids into his web of deceit. He was never impatient; he gave a little and would then sign off but only after scheduling another chat for the next day with the Chavez kids.

This is how I came to know the Chavez kids. I received the recorded transcripts of their conversation with Rivas and knew immediately that Rivas was up to no good again. Rivas was not an unknown entity to me. I had busted him and put him in prison for his first sex crime.

I have to tell you here that a child predator is one of the sickest of mental patients. They are helpless fighting the urges that cause their predation and it is not easy treating them. I have had sexual predators plead with me to kill them so that they would not prey on anyone ever again.

The human mind NEVER gives up anything sensual and as any sex addict will tell you, sexual addiction is a horrible disease that destroys the victims as well as the perpetrator. It is all about lust; lust needs to be renewed and renewed with a bigger thrill and more depraved.

Take for instance a 14-year old teen age boy who has his frist glimpse of naked women in a Playboy magazine. He delights in what he sees and fantasizes. His hormones are raging and left unchecked his lust will seek a bigger thrill.

When pornographic images aren't enough, he seeks to have sex with teenage girls. You only need to see the statistics on this problem to understand how prevalent this has become.

When teenage sex isn't enough, he seeks out older prostitutes and where do you think he gets the money for this?

As he grows older, prostitutes do not give him a bigger thrill so he adds violence into the mix. The prostitutes now avoid him so he forcibly takes what he wants and now he has become a rapist.

When rape is enough he begins a life of murder and we now have a serial killer on our hands. Step by step into depravity, spiraling down into the pit and all because his addiction was left unchecked.

This is what happened to Rivas. As the Latino kids taunted him, he began to physically fight back. He was a big kid and hurt a good many kids so they expelled him from school. To pass the time he used his parent's computer. He became self-taught on the computer and quickly learned he could remain anonymous and that no one knew he was an epileptic. For once in Rivas' life, he felt empowered and this soon became his addiction.

Rivas' first victim was a 13-year old girl that he first befriended in a teen chat room and as their relationship progressed Rivas told her that he loved her and wanted to meet her. Rivas drove to her town and they met outside of a bowling alley.

Rivas used all of his alluring powers on this innocent and naive girl and soon they both were back at his motel where he brutally sodomized her and raped her. He then left her there but not before threatening her that if she told anyone anything he would return and kill her and her family.

The girl refused to speak to the police for fear for her life and her family and the case was soon closed for lack of cooperation. Her parents however were determined to find the guy that brutalized their daughter so my company ForensicsNation.com was hired to track Rivas down.

In reviewing the computer logs on their daughter's computer I discovered where she had been chatting and it was obvious that the one chat room where she had spent most of her time was the one where she had met Rivas.

I admit that I missed the fact that the chat room where they had met was a Latino chat room and I also overlooked the fact that Rivas' first victim was Latina. In my interview with his first victim, she kept repeating the fact that he said he loved her.

With the chat room's permission I planted a software bug and programmed it to notify me of any conversation that had the word love in it. I was swamped with transcripts so I went back to his first victim for more clues. This is where Rivas slipped up and this is how I caught him.

Rivas had told his first victim that he had a Camero and that he had rebuilt it personally so that it was fast. I reprogrammed the software with the word Camero and had 31-hits immediately and all from the same user "FastBoy" talking to young Latina girls.

I investigated this user "FastBoy" to discover his location. As I suspected he was using offshore proxies to hide his true identity. I then planted a software program into the chat room's server that when FastBoy logged in again, this program would plant itself in FastBoy's computer and transmit his location.

I didn't have long to wait; the very next day FastBoy logged in and I now knew his name and address. Although television romanticizes cops and investigators, the truth is the main part of the job is waiting patiently to watch your target and gather evidence. This is what forensics is about; the compilation and preservation of evidence so that you can put the dirtbag behind bars.

I watched FastBoy for two weeks and saw that his modus operendi (MO) was identical to his first victim. He said he loved his victim and then set up a meeting. I allowed him to do this with three Latina girls and then notified law enforcement and presented the evidence.

Rivas met his second victim in a large west coast city and was unaware that he was being tracked and followed. When he rented a secluded motel room and entered it with his second victim, law enforcement moved in and arrested him.

In a line-up, his first victim identified him and Rivas was convicted of child endangerment, sodomy, and a bunch of other charges too numerous to list. He was sentenced to 10-years in prison and served five. When he was released, he was required to register as a sex offender, which he did.

Armed with the knowledge now that he targeted only Latino kids in Latino chat rooms, it was pretty easy to keep track of Rivas' online activities.

When I read the transcripts of his conversation with Reuben and Sonya, I immediately notified law enforcement and brought them up to date on what Rivas was planning.

Rivas' initial meeting with Reuben and Sonya was at the Internet café in Ensenada. He convinced them that he could smuggle them into the United Sates and then get them their "green cards". When they asked the cost; he quoted them $5,000 but that he could wait until they were employed and then they could pay him $100/month each.

Again Rivas was unaware that he was being watched and recorded although he was a good deal more careful than the first time. The video showed a nervous man constantly scanning his surroundings.

Rivas set up the next meeting date and told the kids to only bring a few clothes. He would smuggle them across the border and then drive them to their parents.

Law enforcement made arrangements with the US Border Patrol to allow Rivas through the border check point so that they could follow him and bust him again just like the first time. Everything went smoothly; they followed Rivas using a helicopter and notified the ground units when he stopped at a secluded motel outside the town of Bakersfield.

Law enforcement again waiting until Rivas brought the Chavez kids into the rented room and then moved in and busted him and rescued the kids. They had no idea of the danger they were in and emotionally became basket cases when they were told what was happening. I made arrangements for their parents to take care of them and spoke to the US Attorney (this was a federal case since he crossed a border with the kids) that prosecuted the case to allow them entry, which he referred over to immigration.

Rivas was convicted at trial and because this was his second conviction, he was given a 25-year sentence. In the Federal system, Rivas had to serve approximately 85% of his sentence. Rivas would be gone a long, long time.

Postscript: The whole Chavez family was eventually deported to Mexico but has applied for legal immigration. Go here to learn how to protect your children:

http://bit.ly/LvOw32

Chapter 4 – Neither Good Enough for Heaven nor Earth

I chose the name of this chapter for a specific reason. In my counseling practice, I have witnessed firsthand the enormous psychological damage that racism causes to the human mind.

The human psyche is fragile enough, but after a continuous frontal assault by racism, it doesn't take long for various types of manifested behavior to rear up and cause havoc.

Self worth is a delicate concept. How we view ourselves falls under a more critical eye than how others view us.

In the Christian faith it says, "Therefore if any man *be* in Christ, *he is* a new creature: old things are passed away; behold, all things are become new." - 2Co 5:17

And although even some people struggle with the belief that God has forgiven them, they are more critical of themselves to a point that they never forgive themselves or let go of the past.

In other words, they are neither good enough for heaven nor earth!

Too late for fruit; too soon for flowers!

What does the statement above mean to you? If it is too late for fruit and too soon for flowers, then it implies a certain kind of limbo.

You must first have flowers in order to obtain fruit and if you are in between both then you are positioned to begin again. Every year a new beginning occurs...a new chance at life as a bleak and dreary winter gives way to the promise and hope of spring. Flowers bloom once again; the death of a seed becomes the life of fruit.

I was born in May. It was a time of renewal; the earth threw off its mantle of white, replacing it with blossoms, signaling the restoration of life. The sun shone its warmth, and the earth awoke to the fulfillment of a promise made by Him. It is never too late for restoration; spring always comes and life renews.

And is the same with YOU!

*****

I met Charlie at a fast food restaurant. I had come in for coffee and to review my case files. He was a short boy with a bad case of acne. He had jet black hair that was straight and thick. At first I thought he was Latino. It turned out that he was a Native American. He was Navajo.

I watched him from the booth where I sat as he worked filling people's orders. He was the kind of kid that people never noticed. They pretty much looked right through him.

The next time I met Charlie was at the local vet's office. I had brought my dog in to have his shots renewed and I saw him through the chain link fence as he cleaned the kennels and played with the dogs.

I could tell he really loved animals and they really loved him. I walked up to the fence and said, "Didn't you serve me coffee the other day?"

He looked up sheepishly, "Why yes, I remember you. Not many people engage me in conversation but I remember you thanking me for the great service."

"I see you like dogs…"

He interrupted, "Oh yes; is that your Yorkie," he motioned to my dog that I was holding.

"Yes; his name is Gage. I brought him in for shots."

"I love Yorkies; they are my favorite breed and I wish I could afford one."

"Would your parents agree for you to have one?" I asked.

"I live by myself; my parents died a few years back and I haven't any relatives." He replied almost embarrassed at his plight. "That's why I work two jobs. But I like to work."

"You are an interesting young man. We will talk again." I said as I turned to leave. "I will most likely see you for coffee."

"Okay…any time…see ya."

I turned to leave and at my car I looked back and saw Charlie wave. I waved back and drove away.

When I got home I called the breeder where I had got Gage and inquired if she had any Yorkie puppies. She did so I bought one…a male… and she drove it over to the vet's office the next day with a card, "You may not be able to afford this little guy but can you afford to be without him?"

A few days later, on a Friday, I went in for more coffee and there was Charlie looking at me with a beaming smile. He was almost in tears as he thanked me for the puppy. He had named it Lobo and I laughed. As we talked I mentioned that I had a picnic to attend the next day and I invited Charlie to go with me. He almost jumped at the invitation and I could tell that he very rarely got out and socialized.

I picked Charlie and Lobo up the next afternoon for the picnic. I had brought Gage with me so the two of them could bond and have some fun together.

Charlie lived behind a hardware store in a very small room. It didn't have a shower; he used the hardware store's washroom to clean up. Candidly, it was pathetic.

He told me that in exchange for cleaning up the store at night the owner let him live in the room in the back. I then asked him how old we was and he told me he was seventeen.

"Why aren't you in school," I asked.

"I dropped out. I needed to support myself and I wasn't good at sports or academics so my needs and school kind of just collided. Anyway, I wasn't very popular with my acne and small size and being an Indian either so it was easier to just drop out. I take a GED course online so I will graduate."

"You have a computer?" I asked.

"No, I use one of the computers at the hardware store. The owner gave me permission."

I nodded as I pulled into the park where the picnic was being held. Charlie and I had a lot of fun at the picnic. He ate a lot and I introduced him to the people I knew and even the young people I worked with on a daily basis. Charlie made some friends that day and thanked me for my kindness. As I dropped him off at his place, he smiled and waved as I pulled away.

I found it difficult to get Charlie off my mind. Racism affects the young too and Charlie was a very young victim.

I marveled at the fact that this boy wasn't bitter; he took life as it came and made the most of it. He didn't socialize because he was well accepted so he worked to get by and make the most of it.

The next time I saw Charlie he was walking from the restaurant to the vet's office. I pulled over and offered him a ride, which he gladly accepted. Although Charlie had a driver's license, which for some reason amazed me, he didn't have a car so he walked the three miles between the restaurant and the vet's office daily and then the four miles from the vet's office back to the hardware store.

I was curious about this boy and asked him what he did for entertainment? His answer really surprised me. "The owner at the hardware store has a TV in his office and I have his permission to watch that but mostly I read."

"What do you like reading," I asked.

"Mostly stuff on gardening and landscaping; I want to be a landscaper so I read everything about it that I can get my hands on…mostly at the library."

"Are you good at it?" I asked.

"I think so, I did all of the flower pots in front of the hardware store and people have commented on them enough that the owner is considering having me do more and selling them."

"Tell me, why don't you get a job with a landscaper?"

Charlie just stared at me with a sad expression on his face. Then he said, "I tried but no one will hire an Indian. I even offered to work for free to just gain the experience but they just laughed at me and said that Indians did not make good landscapers. I have no idea what they meant by that."

"I looked over at Charlie, "People can be real jerks, Charlie. Let me look around and I will see what I can do."

A good friend of mine named John Petry owned a lawn maintenance business in a couple of towns over from where I lived. I called him and told him about Charlie. John owed me a favor; he had once had a drinking problem that I helped him kick.

I told John that Charlie didn't have a car and that I would drive him over for an interview. John said Charlie could use one of the company trucks if he hired him.

A few days later I drove Charlie over for his interview and John liked him immediately. I was amazed at how much Charlie had learned from his books and John was amazed that having never worked in lawn maintenance, Charlie knew a good deal about it.

Charlie got hired and was given a company truck. He was able to quit his two other jobs and he began as low man mowing lawns. Charlie worked hard and John was quite pleased with him.

In the course of his employment with John, Charlie showed him some of the flower arrangements that he had done for the hardware store. John was very impressed. He had Charlie created a dozen arrangements, which John sold through his business. The sales were very lucrative; enough so that John decided to open a separate business putting Charlie in charge of creating arrangements.

Business was very good; Charlie was soon hiring people to help him. Most of his arrangements were for outside pots and were decorative pieces lining walkways, patios, and gazebos.

A year after Charlie went to work for John, the new business surpassed the lawn maintenance business in income and Charlie moved to be closer to the business. I kept in touch with Charlie for a little while until he moved and then contact between us became less and less.

One day I got a call from Charlie that literally stunned me. John had fired him because he had fallen in love with his daughter and John didn't want any half breed kids in his family. John's daughter wanted to get married and John had adamantly said no.

Charlie was good enough to make John a rich man but not good enough to become a son-in-law. I asked Charlie what he was going to do and he said he had saved his money and was going to open his own business. He also said that John's daughter and he would get married but he would prefer doing it with John's blessing. He then asked me if I would speak to John.

I met John at his office and I quickly could see that he wasn't a happy man. Nothing I said would change John's mind; he was fixed on disowning both his daughter and Charlie if they married. John's wife was in favor of the marriage; she too was upset at John but even she could not sway him from his prejudice.

Charlie and John's daughter did marry and John did disown both of them. Charlie opened his own business and it quickly became successful. John and his wife constantly fought over their daughter and Charlie and it got so bad that they separated.

In the weeks that followed I learned that John had gone back to drinking so it didn't surprise me when I received a call that john had been in an accident and was in intensive care at the hospital.

When I arrived at the hospital, Charlie, his wife and her mother were there. I sat them all down and told them that they had done nothing wrong. This was John's problem and he was attempting to solve it in a bottle using Charlie and his daughter as an excuse.

They needed to understand the truth and do what Charlie had been doing all along – stepping around the bigotry and racism and getting on with their lives. They were never going to be able to convince John and John would continue to use them as an excuse.

I then told them all to go home and let things play out as they would.

Racism and bigotry claims many victims. Charlie lived his life neither good enough for heaven nor earth but learned to step around it. The reality of the situation is ironic. Charlie was the type of man that really was good enough for both.

Postscript: John recovered from his accident but continued to drink. Two months to the day after the accident, John committed suicide. There was no suicide note but police found a little Indian doll with a knife through its heart.

Chapter 5 – The Last Thing to Die in a Man

The last thing to die in a man is pride. Even on the bed called death, a man can shake his angry fist heavenward because the act of physically dying means simply an end to life. There was one infamous man in history that literally shook his fist at God and then died. Do you know who he was? Read on…

A man carefully jumps down from the train platform on a chilly and blustery morning in Chicago. He has come from his native Russia in search of this man they call Jesus. He quickly walks to his stated destination frequently looking down at the paper in his glove-covered hands with its hastily drawn map and address scrawled in almost illegible script. The man gazes up at the church and admires its pointed steeple. He reads on the church directory that Sunday school is just starting so he carefully makes his way inside bowing with an exaggerated politeness to everyone that takes the time to greet the stranger. He finds, much to his dismay that the teacher does not show up. But much more disappointing is the fact that nobody seems to care that the class has been canceled. The man then returns to the sanctuary and waits for the morning worship service to begin but afterwards he is left with a feeling of apathy since no one seemed to be paying attention or listening to the sermon's words. Disgusted, the man turns and leaves. When he returns to his native Russia, this man would find an object worthy of his worship. He would go on to become the Minister of Defense of the Soviet Communist Party. This man was Leon Trotsky.

Another man from Russia stands rigid and stiff as his mother cries and his abusive father just stares off into the distance, seething with anger. He has just informed the both of them that he was expelled as a seminary student in the Russian Orthodox faith. He laments to them that his studies are boring and of little interest to him. To this man, religion is for the weak. Although the young man's news literally breaks his parent's hearts, he remains firm in his beliefs and leaves his studies to pursue a more ambitious goal. This man would go on to become one of the most notorious murderers the world has ever known. This man was Josef Stalin and he is the one who literally shook his fist at God and then died.

A little closer to home in the suburbs of Dallas, Texas, two brothers are brought before the governing board of elders of their church. Their rowdy behavior and disruptive pranks can no longer be tolerated. The older brother's teacher asks the governing board for a little more time to work with the boy. Because of his request, the older brother is given another chance. He will go on to later become the leader of his denomination's evangelical program in the State of Florida. The younger brother is not so fortunate. His teacher recommends expulsion and the governing board agrees and expels the boy from the church. This young man would become world renown for in November 1963 he assassinated the President of the United States, John F. Kennedy. This man was Lee Harvey Oswald.

*****

I am a voracious reader. In the books I read, and the novels I write, I see my own dilemmas, as well as others, come to life. In Nathaniel Hawthorne's, *The Scarlet Letter,* one such character strikes me hard and sends a verbose blow of words to my heart. He is the Puritan minister, Reverend Arthur Dimmesdale; he is a tortured and polluted soul, for he is an adulterer. Like many of his kind, he desires, at all cost, to conceal his sin, for his desire to lead his flock combines with his misdeeds, and communes into guilt without relief. In other words, the Reverend Dimmesdale is a FRAUD!

He screams his dilemma into the face of complicity, "What can a ruined soul like mine affect towards the redemption of other souls, or a polluted soul, towards their purification?" I studied his words for hours. Something about his lamentation did not sit right with me. As I struggled to find the light of his cry, it finally dawned on me that the Reverend Dimmesdale struggled with the reality that he needed to offer his flock, an example, and he could not because he was a polluted soul. However, in his struggle with this reality of guilt, he excluded from his thoughts the possibility of offering them a redeemer. Interesting dilemma, eh?

I was and am a polluted soul too. I, too committed many sins, and paid a heavy price. But, are my sins a barrier to teach, or an example of the forgiving and loving mercy of the Creator who found me and healed me? When I ask myself this question, "Who Am I?" I see only a sinner, redeemed from his sin and given a chance to give back that which I have taken. I am not important, but my message and my Redeemer are!

I am like a jar of clay, the outward appearance rather dull and earthen. I am fragile and weak and all that is good is on the inside, for Life is what goes into the body. The treasure lies within, not on the outside; how often have I looked on the outside? What an odd concept, to be entrusted with the Truth, when I am a broken pot of little earthly value. Could it be that I am chosen as a messenger, a new 21st century Reverend Dimmesdale, someone so lowly who will not detract from the message? If all I have done is impress you and turned your eyes on me, then I have failed, for there is a higher Truth and a nobler impression. A slave is never greater than his master.

It has happened once again; what the world says is the opposite of the truth. The world says that weakness and one's own failings are like a deathblow. The truth says that it will serve to tell the message; the weakest of them all will speak about the strongest message of all time.

Many of you, who read this, will be broken vessels, alone with dark thoughts and anguished hearts. With vengeful hearts, you will want to cry out for justice and relief. The one who hurt you must pay; justice cries out in a voice stronger than you. "It's a pity that God does not remove this despicable person from the earth. Why should he/she be allowed to continue to hurt and deceive?" you may say.

But, I respond as did Nathaniel Hawthorne, "Pity? It was pity that stayed the hand of God. Those possessed by evil are to be pitied. Is there hope for them? Are they to be crushed or restored? If a heart can be mended, cannot they be healed too? If pity stands, without justice, then an evil person's condition could be ignored as being slight, or indifferent."

At what point do we give up on an evil person? If the person were so filled with evil, where he no longer makes choices, but becomes his/her choice, he/she would be beyond hope. The battle is for the hearts and minds of men and women. The great deceiver uses the mind as the battlefield.

So who are you... a broken pot, a lost person, an evil thief of love?

I believe in miracles...

*****

Reginald Thurston Buchwald III was a prideful man. I met him quite by accident on a blustery day in February.

There is a stream that flows out of the mountains where I live. It flows fast and the city had turned a little sliver of land next to it into a park. I often took my dog Gage here to play ball with him because it was peaceful and the sound of the flowing water was therapeutic. And usually I am the only one there.

On this particular day in February, I noticed the expensive sports car in the parking lot and then a man sitting off to the side on a park bench.

As I approached, I nodded my hello and he nodded back as I began throwing the ball for Gage. Suddenly the man spoke, "Do you know what the worst thing in man is? He asked.

I responded, "You would have to give me at the least a couple of days just to answer that question, sir. I am a behavioral scientist; I see quite a lot of broken humanity."

The man got up and walked over to me. Gage impatiently jumped up and down wanting me to throw the ball and quite perplexed at the interruption.

"I just bought a company just to shut it down because it was my main competitor. By doing so I just threw over 800 hundred people out of work. My board of directors said that it was a wise move; I am not so sure so I have been sitting here wondering."

I studied the man for a little while. "I think you know the answer but refuse to face it," I said. "Judging by the sports car in the parking lot, you don't need the money.

So tell me, how much is enough and what is more important; people or money?"

He smiled, "You must be a very good doctor," he began. "I ask myself that question quite often but I still continue to build empires. I think I do it because there are no more frontiers for me to conquer. I have accomplished too much in my life."

I laughed, "You seem to have conquered everything but yourself." I began. "In your mind you have to serve your shareholders; they are more important than the people. Capitalism is a machine of greed and its fuel is profit. It may not be your fault; in capitalism someone that has made a killing in stocks doesn't ever consider that for him/her to make that killing, someone else had to have taken a bloodbath. The system is inherently greedy. It only takes and never gives back."

Reginald really perked up at my words. "I am bound by law to maximize shareholder value. What can I do?"

"The way you operate now, you take and give nothing back. Why not try the opposite – give to get?" I counseled. "By making people first rather than profit, I think you will find that you will make more money."

"That doesn't make sense but yet it does. If the people are happy then they will work harder and our brands will increase. But will my board go along with me?" he wondered out loud.

"I have a rather worn out saying, 'Hunting is for fools who have never heard about bait.' Right now you hunt for customers; try baiting them instead."

"Oh that is really interesting. How do I do that?"

"By giving them more than they expect! The operative word here is GIVING!"

Gage began barking and growling; his tiny little patience had come to an end and he began to growl his frustration at me.

Reginald thanked me and we exchanged business cards and I quickly...really quickly...forgot about Reginald Thurston Buchwald III and never expected to hear from him again.

Postscript: Thirteen months later I received a letter from Reginald and a rather large check as a thank you for our conversation. His letter said that his board of directors balked at his new give to get idea so he fired all of them and appointed employees from different departments. He then but in a bonus plan based on production and profit and made it known that his company would be known for giving to get. The results of his experiment were an increase in profits of over 22% and a reduction of costs by almost 5%. His people are happy and he doesn't do anything without consulting his employee-run board. They give him the human perspective and it works.

Conclusion

I am of the knowledge and belief that bigotry and racism will never end. There is too much profit in it. Ideology be damned; ideology follows the money. This is true in racism, bigotry, hated and more.

In science we use a term called "First Cause". A cocaine addict is not an addict because he/she uses cocaine. That is the effect and not the cause. The First Cause needs to be discovered. Why does a person choose to self-medicate themselves using cocaine? Once this cause is discovered, a treatment protocol can be used to wean a person off of cocaine.

But the battle fighting bigotry and racism begin with each one of us. And the battle is worth fighting. I do my own thinking; I do not allow the mainstream "biased" media to do my thinking anymore than I allow the hate sellers such as Al Sharpton and Jesse Jackson and the NAACP to do my thinking. I am not into sound-bites; I am into facts and I use these objective facts to form my opinions and beliefs.

DO YOUR OWN THINKING! Do not allow anything to shape YOU but objective facts. The Internet abounds with opinions, false information and just plain garbage. Be careful what you allow into your five senses and evaluate all input carefully. Remember, you are what you believe!

I would like to thank my readers and let them know I appreciate them. Whether you read my stuff to learn a different take on a subject or are just fed up with the mainstream media and ever present sound bites, it is my desire to provide you with information so that you can think for yourself instead of others doing your thinking for you.

Write to me and let me know your thoughts: lee.benton@neternatives.com

Blessings to you all!

I Have a Special Gift for My Readers

I appreciate my readers for without them I am just another author attempting to make a difference. If my book has made a favorable impression please leave me an honest review. Thank you in advance for you participation.

My readers and I have in common a passion for the written word as well as the desire to learn and grow from books.

My special offer to you is a massive ebook library that I have compiled over the years. It contains hundreds of fiction and non-fiction ebooks in Adobe Acrobat PDF format as well as the Greek classics and old literary classics too.

In fact, this library is so massive to completely download the entire library will require over 5 GBs open on your desktop.

Use the link below and scan all of the ebooks in the library. You can select the ebooks you want individually or download the entire library.

The link below does not expire after a given time period so you are free to return for more books rather than clog your desktop. And feel free to give the link to your friends who enjoy reading too.

I thank you for reading my book and hope if you are pleased that you will leave me an honest review so that I can improve my work and or write books that appeal to your interests.

Okay, here is the link…

http://tinyurl.com/special-readers-promo

PS: If you wish to reach me personally for any reason you may simply write to mailto:support@epubwealth.com.

I answer all of my emails so rest assured I will respond.

Meet the Author

Dr. Leland Benton is Director of Applied Web Info, a holding company for ePubWealth.com, a leading ePublisher company based in Utah. With over 21,000 resellers in over 22-countries, ePubWealth.com is a leader in ePublishing, book promotion, and ebook marketing.

As the creator and author of "The ePubWealth Program," Leland teaches up-and-coming authors the ins-and-outs of today's ePublishing world. He has assisted hundreds of authors make it big in the ePublishing world.

Leland also created a series of external book promotion programs and teaches authors how to promote their books using external marketing sources.

Leland is also the Managing Director of Applied Mind Sciences, the company's mind research unit and Chief Forensics Investigator for the company's ForensicsNation unit. He is active in privacy rights through the company's PrivacyNations unit and is an expert in survival planning and disaster relief through the company's SurvivalNations unit.

Leland resides in Southern Utah.

Visit some of his websites
http://www.AddMeInNow.com
http://www.AppliedMindSciences.com
http://www.BookbuilderPLUS.com
http://www.BookJumping.com
http://www.EmailNations.com
http://www.EmbarrassingProblemsFix.com
http://www.ePubWealth.com
http://www.ForensicsNation.com
http://www.ForensicsNationStore.com
http://www.FreebiesNation.com
http://www.HealthFitnessWellnessNation.com
http://www.Neternatives.com
http://www.PrivacyNations.com
http://www.RetireWithoutMoney.org
http://www.SurvivalNations.com
http://www.TheBentonKitchen.com
http://www.Theolegions.org
http://www.VideoBookbuilder.com

Some Other Books You May Enjoy From ePubWealth.com, LLC Library Catalog

EPW Library Catalog Online
http://www.epubwealth.com/wp-content/uploads/2013/07/Leland-benton-private-turbo.pdf

EPW Library Catalog Download
http://www.filefactory.com/f/562ef3ea1a054f0a

.

www.ingramcontent.com/pod-product-compliance
Lightning Source LLC
Chambersburg PA
CBHW060217290526
45789CB00003B/1300